VIEWS

SEATTLE AND THE PUGET SOUND

EMERALD POINT PRESS

ISBN 0-9637816-5-0

Copyright © 2002
Emerald Point Press, Seattle, Washington

Library of Congress Catalog Card Number: 95-60449

Cover:
Seattle viewed from Kerry Park on Queen Anne Hill
Chris Jacobson

Printed in Hong Kong

It is the artists interpretation of reality, that help us view life, in perspectives that we otherwise may not see. These views of Seattle and the Puget Sound, were all produced by Seattle area photographers. These seasonal images, capture forever, that moment in time, when all forces necessary to create perfection converge.

The city and landscape photographs reproduced in this book, were created by: Bill Brooksher, Dan Carow, John S. Chao, Adrienne DeLiso, Joe Faulkner, Neal Herbert, Chris Jacobson, S.H. Marti, Joe Poehlman, and John Rizzo.

Their artistic vision is yours to enjoy.

▲

SOUTH OF RUBY BEACH—OLYMPIC NATIONAL PARK SEASHORE

Adrienne DeLiso

John S. Chao

TULIP FIELDS–SKAGIT VALLEY

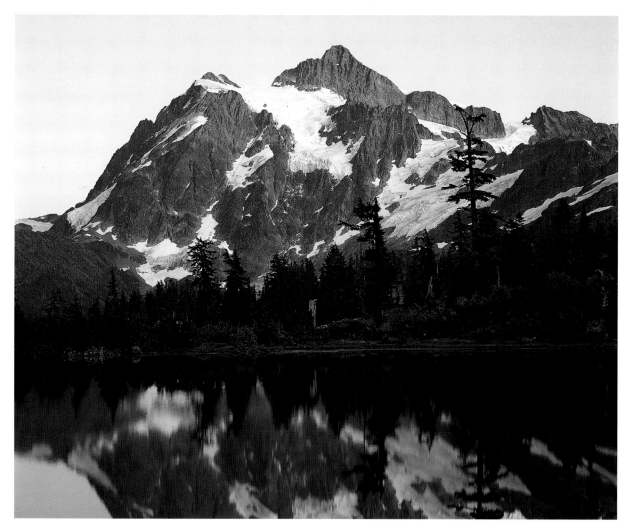

MOUNT SHUKSAN VIEWED FROM PICTURE LAKE—MOUNT BAKER WILDERNESS

Chris Jacobson

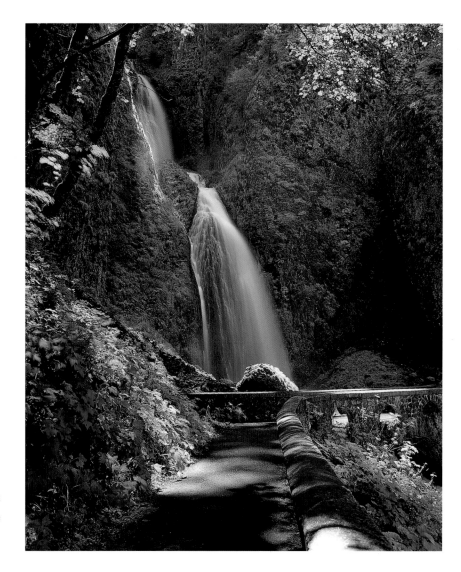

WAHKEENA FALLS—COLUMBIA RIVER GORGE

Chris Jacobson

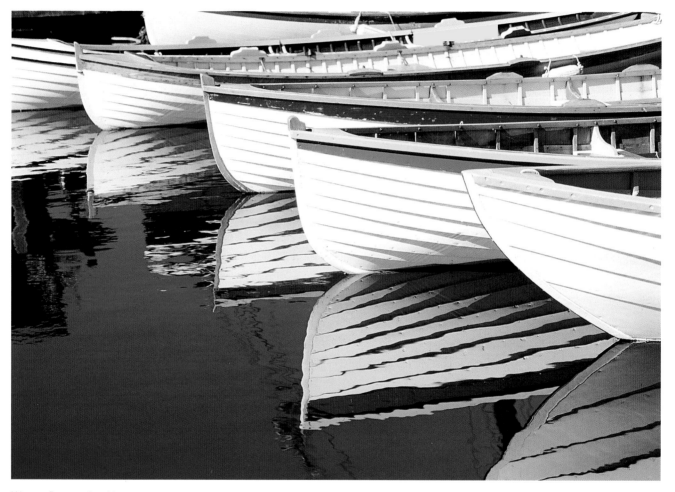

WOODEN BOATS ON LAKE UNION

Chris Jacobson

Joe Poehlman

OLYMPIC MOUNTAINS VIEWED FROM THE PUGET SOUND

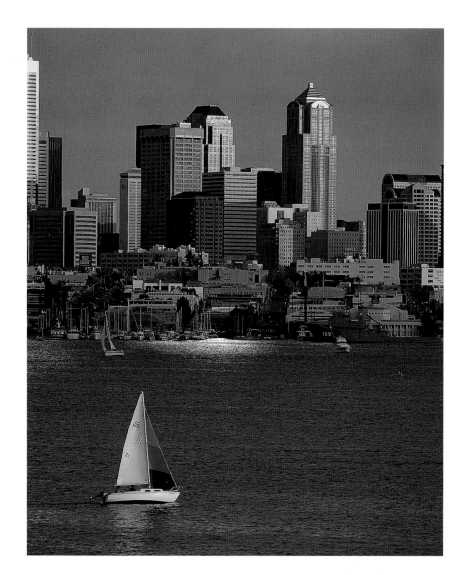

SEATTLE VIEWED FROM LAKE UNION

Chris Jacobson

Chris Jacobson

DAFFODIL FIELDS–MOUNT VERNON

MOUNT SHUKSAN–MOUNT BAKER WILDERNESS

Joe Poehlman

John S. Chao

SEATTLE AT DUSK VIEWED FROM THE SOUTH

Joe Poehlman

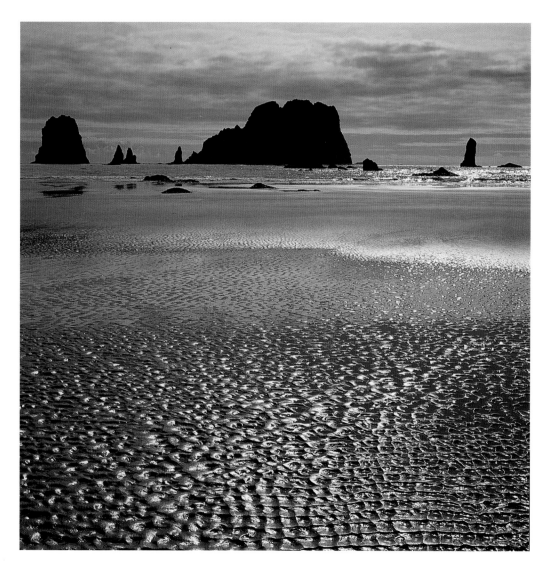

SEA STACKS
OLYMPIC NATIONAL PARK SEASHORE

Neal Herbert

VIEW FROM HURRICANE RIDGE—OLYMPIC NATIONAL PARK

Dan Carow

Chris Jacobson

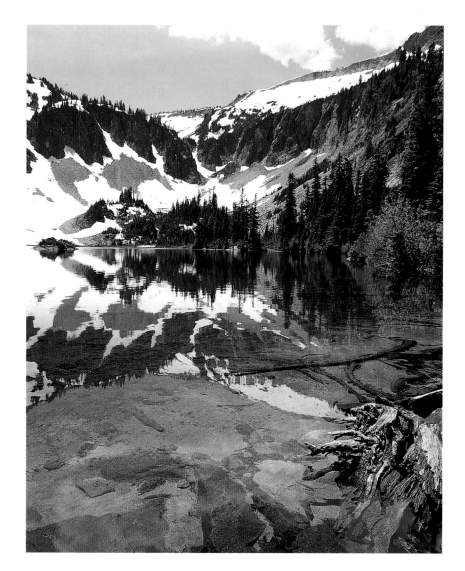

Snow Lake—Mount Rainier National Park

Chris Jacobson

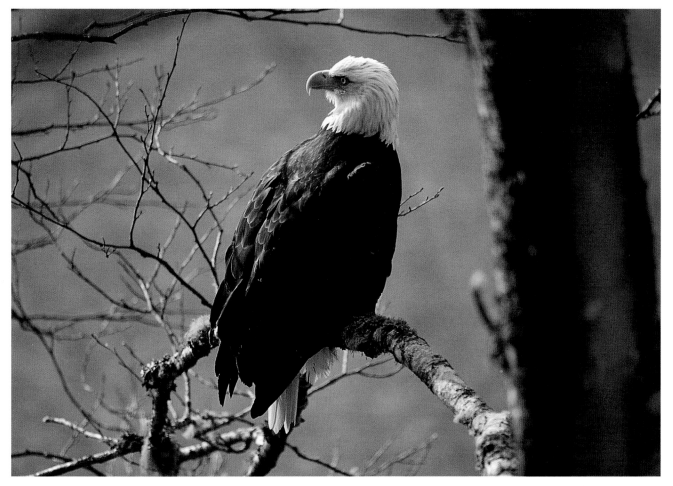

Adrienne DeLiso

BALD EAGLE–SKAGIT RIVER

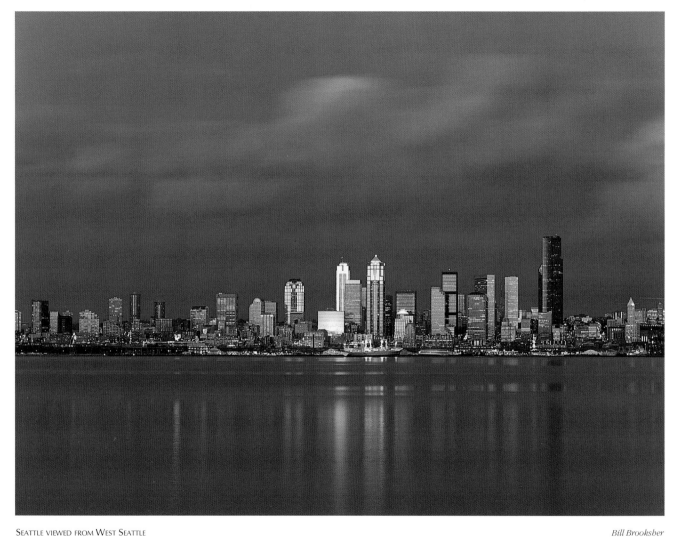

SEATTLE VIEWED FROM WEST SEATTLE

Bill Brooksher

Bill Brooksher

21

FISHERMAN'S TERMINAL—SEATTLE

Bill Brooksher

Chris Jacobson

TULIP GARDENS—MOUNT VERNON

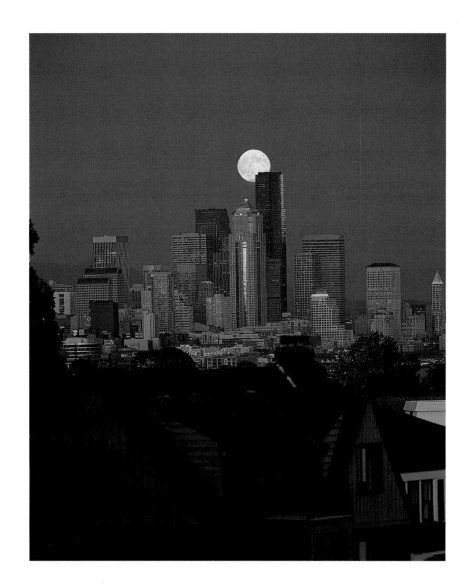

MOONRISE IN SEATTLE FROM MAGNOLIA PARK

Chris Jacobson

Chris Jacobson

NORTHWEST WASHINGTON COASTLINE

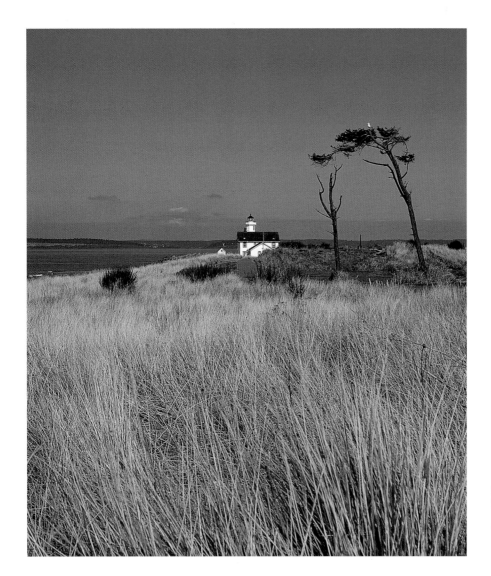

POINT WILSON LIGHTHOUSE
FORT WORDEN STATE PARK

Adrienne DeLiso

Joe Faulkner

EDMONDS FERRY AND OLYMPIC MOUNTAINS

Joe Poehlman

John S. Chao

SOURCE LAKE STREAM—SNOQUALMIE PASS

FIREWORKS OVER LAKE UNION

S.H. Marti

Chris Jacobson

TULIP GARDENS—MOUNT VERNON

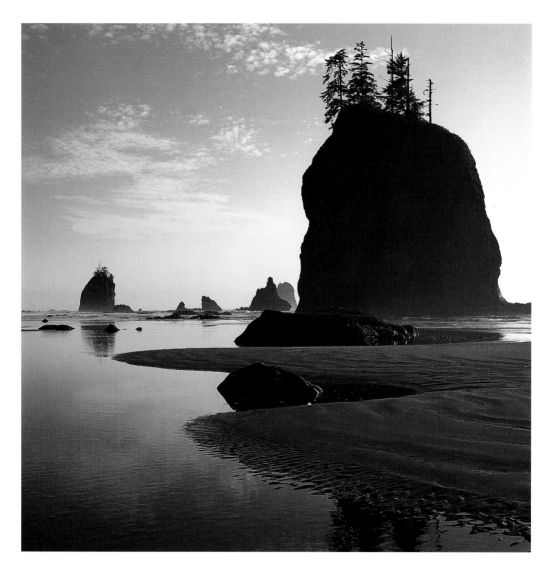

SEA STACKS
OLYMPIC NATIONAL PARK
SEASHORE

Neal Herbert

Bill Brooksher

KUBOTA GARDENS IN AUTUMN

Bill Brooksher

Bill Brooksher

NORTH HEAD LIGHTHOUSE—COLUMBIA RIVER

S.H. Marti

Chris Jacobson

MOUNT RAINIER VIEWED FROM REFLECTION LAKES—MOUNT RAINIER NATIONAL PARK

Winter Evening in Seattle viewed from Queen Anne Hill

Bill Brooksher

S.H. Marti

MOUNT RAINIER VIEWED FROM REFLECTION LAKES—MOUNT RAINIER NATIONAL PARK

VIEW FROM MAGNOLIA PARK

Joe Faulkner

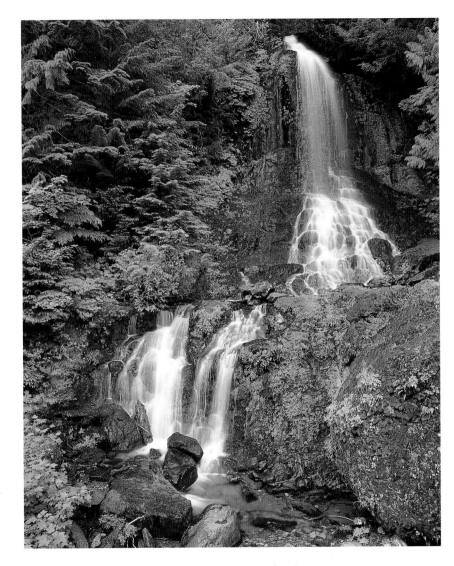

FALLS CREEK FALLS NEAR OHANAPECOSH
MOUNT RAINIER NATIONAL PARK

Chris Jacobson

Fall Leaves—Washington Park Arboretum

Chris Jacobson

John S. Chao

JAPANESE GARDEN—WASHINGTON PARK ARBORETUM

Joe Poehlman

Chris Jacobson

CRYSTAL FALLS IN WINTER–MOUNT RAINIER NATIONAL PARK

FISHERMAN'S TERMINAL—SEATTLE

Bill Brooksher

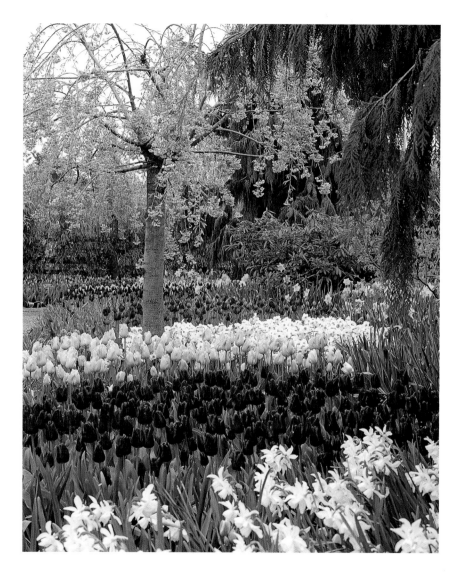

TULIP GARDENS
MOUNT VERNON

Chris Jacobson

Mount Shuksan in Winter viewed from Picture Lake—Mount Baker Wilderness

S.H. Marti

S.H. Marti

Mount Shuksan in Fall viewed from Picture Lake—Mount Baker Wilderness

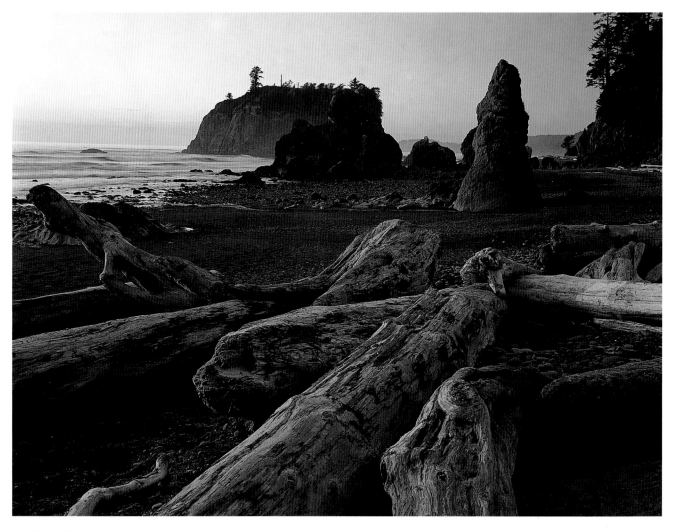

RUBY BEACH—OLYMPIC NATIONAL PARK SEASHORE

Bill Brooksher

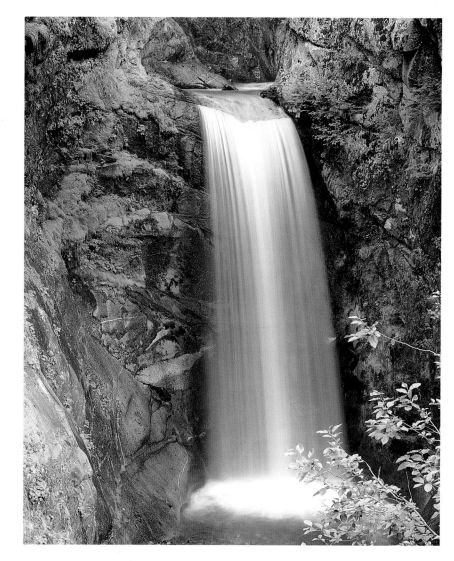

CRYSTAL FALLS
MOUNT RAINIER NATIONAL PARK

Chris Jacobson

SEATTLE VIEWED FROM KERRY PARK ON QUEEN ANNE HILL

Chris Jacobson

Adrienne DeLiso

EBEY'S LANDING—WHIDBEY ISLAND

Joe Poehlman

Chris Jacobson

JAPANESE GARDEN–WASHINGTON PARK ARBORETUM

55

SEATTLE VIEWED FROM HARBOR ISLAND

S.H. Marti

Chris Jacobson

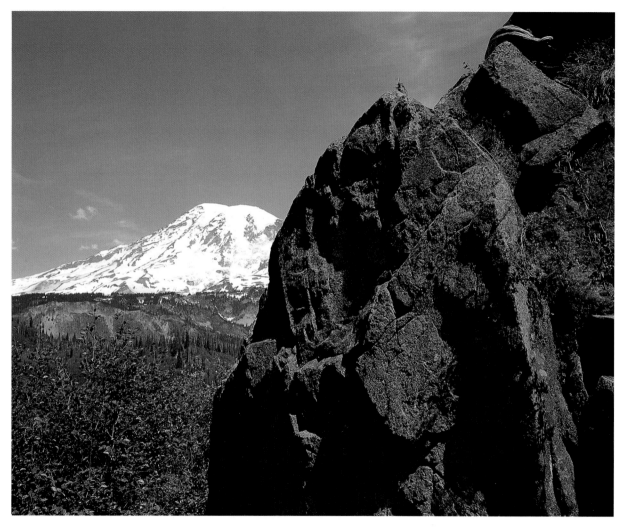

MOUNT RAINIER VIEWED FROM THE SNOW LAKE TRAIL—MOUNT RAINIER NATIONAL PARK

Chris Jacobson

HOH RAIN FOREST
OLYMPIC NATIONAL PARK

Neal Herbert

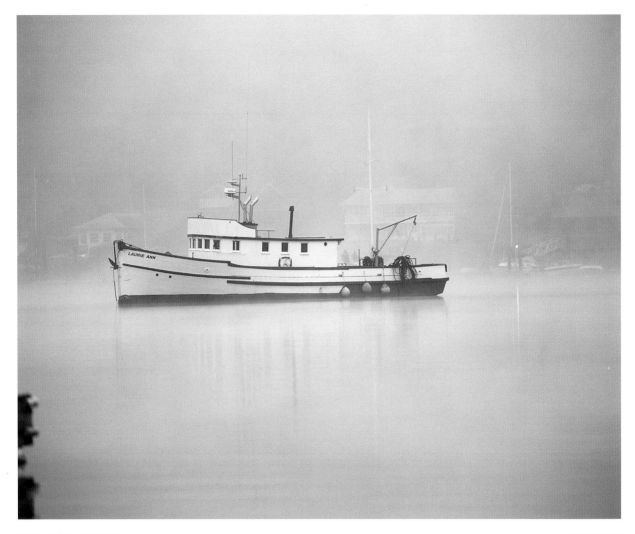

FISHING BOAT—GIG HARBOR

Chris Jacobson

SEA STACKS—NORTH RIALTO BEACH—OLYMPIC NATIONAL PARK SEASHORE

SEATTLE AT SUNSET VIEWED FROM WEST SEATTLE

Bill Brooksher

John Rizzo